AF594754

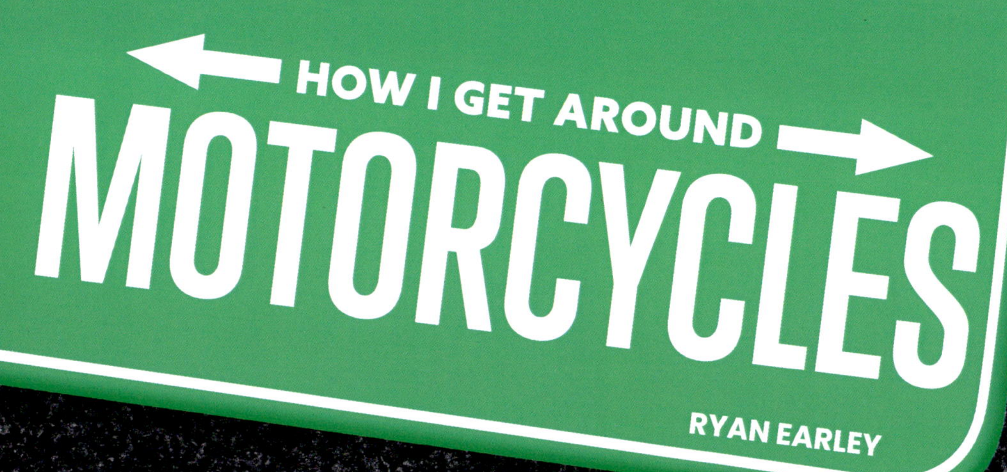


# TABLE OF CONTENTS

Sight Words.......................................2

Words to Know.................................3

Index...................................................16

A Pelican Book

## Teaching Tips for Caregivers and Teachers:

Research shows that one of the best ways for students to learn a new topic is to read about it.

### Before Reading

- Read the title and predict what the book will be about.
- Read the "Words to Know" and discuss the meaning of each word.
- Read the back cover to see what the book is about.

### During Reading

- When a student gets to a word that is unknown, ask them to look at the rest of the sentence to find clues to help with the meaning of the unknown word.
- Motivate students with praise and encouragement.

### After Reading

- Discuss the main idea of the book.
- Ask students to give one detail that they learned in the book.

## Sight Words

all
around
by
get
go
have
I
most
on
the
two

# Words to Know

engines

handlebars

lights

motorcycle

road

wheels

I get around by **motorcycle**.

motorcycle

All motorcycles have **engines**.

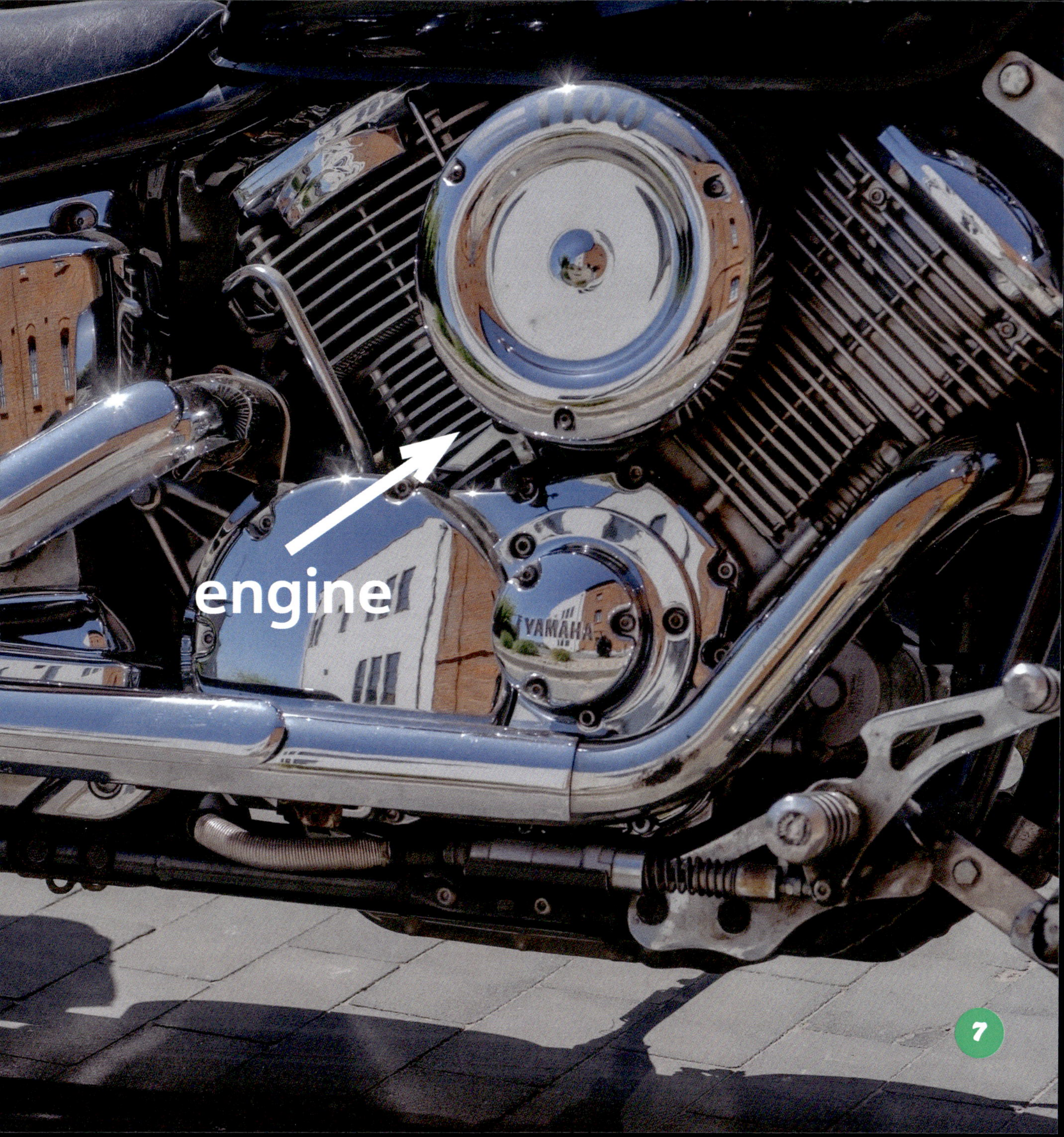
engine

Most motorcycles have two **wheels**.

wheel
SPYKE
ZENO
MOTO

handlebar

All motorcycles have **handlebars**.

Most motorcycles have **lights**.

light

Most motorcycles go on the **road**.

road

# Index

engines 6, 7
handlebars 10, 11
lights 12, 13
road 14, 15
wheels 8, 9

Written by: Ryan Earley
Design by: Niko Magaro
Editor: Kim Thompson
Series Development: James Earley

Photos: All images from Shutterstock

**Library of Congress PCN Data**
Motorcycles / Ryan Earley
How I Get Around
ISBN 979-8-8945-9261-9(hard cover)
ISBN 979-8-8945-9275-6(paperback)
ISBN 979-8-8945-9303-6(EPUB)
ISBN 979-8-8945-9289-3(eBook)
ISBN 979-8-8945-9317-3(audio)
ISBN 979-8-8945-9331-9(Read-Along)
Library of Congress Control Number: 2024946364

Printed in Canada/012025/CP20250101

**Seahorse Publishing Company**
seahorsepub.com



**Published in the United States**
**Seahorse Publishing**
PO Box 771325
Coral Springs, FL 33077